Forewarned
Is
Forearmed

Debbie Digby

Your Guide to Professional
Hairdressing Services &
Sound Procedures

With Relevant Case Studies

Praise for Debbie Digby's Work

Debbie Digby is an industry inspiration, and what she doesn't know isn't worth knowing! I have known her for 22 years and her wealth of experience and latest knowledge has been invaluable to me; I call her DD24/7! Debbie has been a guide and mentor to me throughout my career and will continue to be, and I'm very proud to also call her my best friend.

Barrie Stephen
Barrie Stephen Group

Debbie Digby is one of those people that you are glad you met the minute she has left the room. Integrity with knowledge and professionalism (Our ability to perform under stress is limited by our knowledge of process and procedures) Debbie has the unique qualities of knowledge of process and procedures and is a Salon Owner / Distributor / World Class Educator which makes her one of the few people in our industry that truly shares facts that are relevant and can be put into use the next day.

Robert Shipton
Industry Veteran

Good business practice, well executed can be relied upon in court. Ultimately Debbie run's a good business and this gave her insurers confidence to defend a spurious claim. Now she applies her talents to inspire and inform others in the hair industry. Her tenacity is greatly admired and this book should be a case study for every level to learn from. I look forward to reading more. Keep it up.

Brian Plunkett
Trichocare

About Debbie Digby

With 40 years experience in the hairdressing industry, Debbie Digby is an expert in success. Her first business began in 1987 and over the last three decades her fascinating journey has taken her all over the world. She was 3.6.5 Salon Education's first female lecturer, and in 2000 became 3.6.5's Director of Education developing business programs for successful salons. She was also involved in developing 365 in Australia and the USA. When Paul Mitchell launched their colour in Europe Debbie was appointed Brand Manager and successfully launched PM The Color into more than 15 European Countries. This led to a period of employment in professional hairdressings largest corporate company, Beauty Systems Group. Realising her heart belongs to the independent hairdressing sector, she left the Corporate world behind and founded Passion4hair, an independent distributor of hair products with an education foundation. Debbie says "I have been so fortunate to work in all aspects of the hairdressing industry. My experience has afforded me the unique position to be able to understand our industry from many different perspectives". Today Debbie is CEO of Passion4hair and maintains her position as Managing Director of Feathers Salon Group. She is passionate about bringing unique solutions to salons.

Acknowledgements

My thanks go out in particular to Brittany Newby, Irma Maijaskaite and Kim Watson, without whom this book would read a different story. Thanks also to Kimberley Levine, Beverley Bates, Marguerite Marshall and salon owners who for one reason or another remain anonymous. You have so graciously shared your experiences with the sole purpose of helping others. Heartfelt thanks to all my employees past and present - you made the journey worthwhile. And lastly proud thanks to my son, Declan, who helped me put the book together from inception to publication. I am truly Grateful.

Dedicated to Mum and Dad

Debbie xoxo

Preface

This book deals with the legal issues hairdressers face when carrying out chemical services. When I received a letter from a no win no fee solicitor itemising 10 actions carried out on their 'client' in my salon that had apparently caused damage to her hair and therefore rendered us negligent, I was mortified. I felt sick. Once I had spoken to the three stylists involved it was apparent to me that we were being wrongly accused. We agreed we wanted to fight the allegations. One of the things that helped me throughout the case was knowing about other cases and having the ability to make comparisons. I am compelled to write this book to share information, give guidance and help build confidence in dealing with matters of a legal nature. Many individuals have assisted me in the writing and researching of this book. Some have chosen anonymity and some are able to put a name to their accounts. Such is the nature of this very difficult subject. Thank you to all who have helped. Without all of you this book would not have been possible. Who could have known 10 years ago that the UK would be leading the World in the professional standards of hairdressing – BY DEFAULT. Yes, we find ourselves in a position where following manufacturers instructions, carrying out health and safety practices and stringently documenting services and procedures are imperative when carrying out hair services. I guess other industries may find this book interesting and helpful too, because we are certainly not the only industry in the UK under scrutiny. I have had contact with some people in the holiday industry and have gathered some interesting information from that industry that will help us gain insight into what is going on and how we could and should be dealing with the challenges. About 8 years ago I was involved in a legal case against a salon and was having a conversation with a commercial lawyer who worked for the NHF. He told me there were many cases he was advising on at the time and I asked him the question "where have all these cases come from suddenly?" I felt confused that practices and procedures I had performed and seen performed in a similar way for over 30 years in salons were now being scrutinised and criticised – and salons were being sued for seemingly senseless reasons. His reply was "unfortunately hairdressing salons are cannon fodder for these no-win no-fee lawyers." "How do you mean?" I asked. "Even if they have done nothing wrong, without any documentation it is difficult to fight a case and therefor insurance companies often have no option than to pay out – that is if the insurance company agree to cover the case." Yes, it was around that time that insurance companies started refusing to cover cases if the manufacturers instructions were not followed. Little did I know at that time, circumstance would lead me to this crusade. I can be contacted by email debbie@passion4hair.com

How To Use This Book

This book has been put together with my beloved hairdressers at heart. I know some of you do not ordinarily read books. Your creativity errs towards other activities and media. However there is important information within these pages you should read and digest. With this in mind, the case studies and testimonies have been printed more or less as they were written to maintain authenticity and simplicity. Chapters 1 - 5 document the case won by Feathers Colchester. This can be read as one story on its own. Chapters 6 - 13 are case studies and can be read in any order and alone. I have referenced the book with headings so that if you are looking for a specific piece of information you might find it by flicking through. The book is a series of events and stories intended to be used as a guide and reference. You don't have to be a dedicated reader to benefit from this book. I sincerely hope you find the information you need. I can be contacted on

debbie@passion4hair.com

Table Of Contents

Hair Industry Regulation? We have it...

In 1978 when I was attending college to obtain my City and Guilds in Hairdressing I specifically remember a local salon owner coming in to talk to us about hairdressing as a career. "You have made a great choice to be a hairdresser" he said – the statement got my attention, it was the first time someone had positively validated my choice of career. For the most part, people around me thought my entry into the hairdressing industry was a poor decision. He went on, "it will not be long before the government regulate our industry and we will be recognised as professionals, the industry is campaigning for it". That was 40 years ago, I have heard the same desire for regulation of our industry over four decades. We have various organisations and I believe we have tried to come together as one body, but still we remain fragmented. Here is what I have come to realise, our industry is regulated...... BUT NOT BY DESIGN. What's more, in many aspects, our industry is failing in that regulatory scrutiny. The no win no fee solicitor and the insurance companies that deal with them on our behalf are regulating our industry by holding us accountable for the services we provide to the general public. *{Regulation is an abstract concept of management of complex systems according to a set of rules and trends. In business industry self-regulation occurs through self-regulatory organisations and trade organisations which allow industries to set rules with less government involvement}.* At this point I want to thank the many people (and it is many – from many aspects of our industry) for your congratulations, good wishes and interest in the case and our WIN against a no-win no-fee solicitor. Also, a massive shout out

to the three employees, Irma Majauskaite, Kim Watson and Brittany Newby who went through this legal process with me – it was harrowing for them but they stood up for what is right. More about them later. I have no doubt that you are reading this because you want to know the details of the case, what you can learn and implement into your business and how you can protect yourself and your business from a spurious claim. I believe that in order to benefit from Feathers Colchester's experience in the matter of winning the case against a no win no fee solicitor, the topic needs to be understood in full. I find, that when trying to understand a principle it is often easier to look outside of our own situation. For this purpose let's look at the holiday industry, you may be aware that they are under attack from bogus claims regarding food poisoning.

In June 2017 the Daily Mail reported that since 2013 insurance claims against holiday companies and hotels involving gastric illness have rocketed with typical payouts between £2000 - £3000 made within months of a claim being lodged. It would appear all that is required to make a claim is a photograph of the anti diarrhea drug Imodium and a simple dated receipt, advises a 'claims tout' who operates at pool sides in popular resorts such as Greece, Turkey, Portugal and Spain. He is paid commission by a UK insurance claims company to recruit holidaymakers who fit the solicitors criteria, with children being popular targets because of the nature of their sensitive tummies. "It is only British people making these claims" Says Jorge Marichal, the owner of several hotels in Tenerife. "They went up 6oo per cent in terms of food related illness claims from 2015-2016, and that is a direct result of the scandalous tactics of these cowboy firms." It is said that 'Gastro-Fraud' is to some degree the successor to whiplash after the claims industry came under pressure following the Government's crackdown on false whiplash injury applications. But hoteliers are not taking this lying down. Two people from Liverpool who claimed they were 'bedridden' because of food poisoning managed to down 109 alcoholic drinks over nine days as recorded by their bill. And for those that find all this a little unpalatable take solace in the news from the five star Caldera Palace Hotel on Crete whose owner refused to submit when a couple from Darlington, County Durham lodged an alleged fake claim and instead, is counter suing for £170000 for injury to the hotel's reputation after the manager produced evidence that the couple consumed large amounts

of alcohol during their supposed confinement.

Can you see similarities in the above to some of the claims that have been brought upon salons? The case studies later in the book show interesting comparisons. Now – in order to protect ourselves we buy insurance, and if/when a letter appears from a solicitor we pass that letter to the insurers so they may protect us. But if we have not complied with the terms and conditions of the policy we may find ourselves in breach or with a void policy. Here is an example from the travel industry.

How Travel Insurers Use Sneaky Get-Outs:

Travel policies can be worthless if you drink or hurt yourself cycling. Holiday makers are being sold travel insurance that is invalidated by common mishaps. Hidden catches in small print can result in travellers not covered if they have an accident during popular activities such as cycling, horse riding or snorkelling. And in some cases, claims have been denied because travellers have drunk alcohol. Experts warn that millions going on holiday have no idea about the exclusions and may face huge costs. Martin James of complaints website Resolve, said "travel insurance companies are renowned for relying on ambiguous contract terms to get out of paying claims. Holiday makers should be particularly wary when using price comparison websites as the cheapest deals often offer the worst cover." In one recent case, a 52-year-old grandmother injured herself falling off a quad bike in Greece. She was left with thousands of pounds in medical bills after her insurer refused to pay out because the policy excluded quad biking in the small print.

Maybe you know someone who has had insurance refused because they have not complied with the regulations regarding skin testing?

We need to appreciate the importance of understanding in full our responsibility for carrying out services and how we comply with our legal obligation. We are obliged to carry out services with due care and attention and supply goods and services fit for purpose mindful of our responsibility to the consumer and the public at large. If this appears to be coming across a little on the heavy side, I make no apologies. This is serious stuff. Most legal cases are based upon negligence and/or the Consumer Credit Act 2015.

Now let's understand precedent;

{Precedent is an earlier event or action that is regarded as an example or guide to be considered in subsequent similar circumstances.} Feathers Colchester case set a precedent, this could be a good or bad thing depending on how you look at it. We won a case against a no-win no-fee who actually boast in their Youtube advert that in their cases against salons, they have never had an insurance company not pay out. They will have to replace that now because not only did the insurance company support the case all the way to court – WE WON! However, take heed, we had 26 pages of evidence that included - skin testing records, strand testing, comprehensive consultations, work methods, photographs, policies, procedures, correspondence, witness statements and four witnesses. That is a precedent which currently, as we will see in the case studies in chapters 6-13, salons are rarely able to meet.

chapter 2

The Winners

DEBBIE DIGBY

> FROM THE SERVICES THEY CARRIED OUT IN THE SALON TO REPRESENTING FEATHERS COLCHESTER IN COURT – I SALUTE THEM.

The heroes in this story are the three stylists who experienced the whole process - the case duration was from Feb 2015 until June 2017. Without Irma Maijaskaite, Kim Watson and Brittany Newby there is no case because there would be no witnesses. Celebrating their contribution in this whole episode is so important for they are role models for every professional in the hair industry. From the services they carried out in the salon to representing Feathers Colchester in court – I salute them. When I received a letter from Mulderrigs solicitors stating that I should pass to the insurers ten accusations of negligence by my employees on 3rd Feb 2015 and 5th Feb 2015, I immediately set about finding out the facts. We have good systems in place and I could not believe what I was reading. When you have six salons you cannot supervise everyone, so you rely on people to follow procedures. My

5

mind jumped to the worse case scenario - please tell me the team did everything right I whispered to myself. Investigation showed that they had followed every procedure, skin test, strand test, documented consultation and method of work. In fact, I gathered 26 pages of evidence that countered the accusations against us. (Essential evidence is revealed in Chapter 3 entitled Shoddy Hairdressing and Poor Procedures) I telephoned the insurance company, "If ever there where a case you were going to pursue this is it", I said "please send your best loss adjuster and we will help him build a defence case". The whole debacle has been a harrowing experience - At the fact finding stage Kim asked me if she would have to go to court? "I doubt it will get that far" I said. When the solicitor asked for dates we were all available to attend court Kim asked me if she would have to speak in court, "don't worry" I said "I will tell the solicitor to have me and Brittany do all the talking". On the day of the trial I picked Kim up from her house at 7.30am, "how long will it take?" she said, "I should think we will be done by lunchtime" I said, "Judges have much more important things than this to deal with". Little did I know that the case would last all day, or that all four of us would be cross examined by a barrister whose job it is to undermine our testimony and discredit us in anyway possible.

IRMA MAJAUSKAITE

I EVEN STOPPED TRAINING BECAUSE I FELT THAT I CAN'T TEACH YOUNG STYLISTS IF I CAN'T DO IT RIGHT MYSELF.

"When I heard there was a case brought out against us, I was very shocked and I took it very personally. Not only was I worried about losing my job, I was worrying about having to pay a lot of money towards the case. I also started doubting my knowledge, skills and being in the hairdressing industry. I even stopped training because I felt that I can't teach young stylists if I can't do it right myself. The most surprising thing was that court took all day. It felt really tense and scary. Especially when the barrister

called my name to witness in front of the Judge. I've never been to court so it felt really overwhelming, I didn't know what to expect. I was surprised the questions the barrister asked me. For a second I felt like I was in a murder case. He tried to catch me on anything and show the Judge that I had no knowledge. The questions were twisted and I really had to think what I was saying before I could answer any of the questions. A couple of the questions that I remember would be him saying that someone else wrote my statement, because my English was good but not on THAT level. That was when I felt that it was being aimed at me personally to show the Judge that I didn't know what I was doing. Other things he said was;

"You didn't follow skin test procedure."

"You didn't do a test piece."

"You changed the formula" (instead of 10 grams used 30 grams of one colour)"

KIM WATSON

THE MOST SURPRISING THING FOR ME WAS HOW FAR THE NO WIN NO FEE SOLICITORS TOOK THE CASE CONSIDERING THE AMOUNT OF EVIDENCE WE HAD.

"It made me feel a bit confused and concerned, also concerned I had not done my job properly. It changed my mood because it was in the back of my mind what may happen. Worry. It was a long process which meant the worry was still in the back of my mind – and the dread of possibly attending court. The most surprising thing for me was how far the no-win no-fee solicitors took the case considering the amount of evidence we had. I felt glad all of the systems we have in place, glad I work for a company who look out for their staff by putting good procedures in place, nervous that the lawyers don't actually understand hairdressing and scared I may say something wrong although I knew I had done nothing wrong, I had followed all procedures fully. It tests your nerves - they put words in your mouth and try *to say you did not do your job fully. It was not a nice experience, in particular telling me I had done something to the hair which I hadn't."*

(They accused both stylists of using straighteners, which they did not – more on this in chapter 3)

BRITTANY NEWBY

"IT HAS ADDED MORE FUEL TO MY FIRE TO MAKE CHANGE IN OUR INDUSTRY AND REALLY TAKE IT BACK

"I cannot believe someone would sue over hair; maybe I could have understood it if we were negligent or I thought we really messed up as a team but on this case specifically we were extremely diligent due to the nature of the clients character. When I read the initial statement many items listed were lies and that is something I can not tolerate. It is unjust to be able to even serve papers based on lies as it stressed all parties involved and they did nothing wrong. I was IRATE! How dare she make false claims? How can we be living in a society that would even let this happen? I was in utter disbelief. I suppose it affected me in two ways. Firstly I became stricter on policies as a manager, and secondly I needed to become more supportive to those involved as it really was affecting the performance of Irma where she did not want to train anymore, and was not as confident as she was previously behind the chair. It has added more fuel to my fire to make change in our industry and really take it back. We are the change makers and deserve to be in a place of high regard. I am really proud of Irma and Kim for going through this and remaining strong and for Debbie to be making this experience vocal and trusting us when we stayed firm that we were in the right. It is so important to have TRUST with those we work and also work on. I think this could be a really important next step to bring to our consultations, and really use our Togetherness and Success with our clients as they are part of our culture and unfortunately the claimant lived outside of it."

The solicitor leading the case called me a couple of times to ensure all the witnesses were still in employment and available. In one of our calls she explained that in many cases the witnesses simply disappear and consequently the case can go no further. You may be wondering why the insurance company did not settle. After all, towards the end of the case the settlement fee had come right down. It got to a point where it was going to cost more to continue to court (even if we won) than to settle the case.
(See note on QOCS – be wary of this if going to court).

'Qualified one-way costs shifting' was introduced for personal injury claims from 1 April 2013. This means that defendants will generally be ordered to pay the costs of successful claimants but, subject to certain exceptions, will not recover their own costs if they successfully defend the claim.

I believe the case became a point of principle for everyone involved, and when one party wobbled, others passion to fight for what is right kept the case moving forward. Leading up to the court date the solicitors wrote to the insurers, 'the insured are passionate about defending the case and the evidence is compelling, counsel advised chances of success are in the order of 70% perhaps slightly higher. I would be content to run the claim to trial.' This was a defining moment –when given the necessary evidence to defend a claim, insurance companies can and will do it. The insurance company, underwriters, loss adjuster and solicitors were fantastic. Lastly in this chapter is a mention for our barrister, Max Archer. I can only describe his defence of our case as amazing. He had clearly done his homework before the case, he listened carefully to us regarding key points, he briefed us in the morning as to what to expect in the courtroom and how to behave (this is imperative, when they say it is about the Judge on the day – it really is) and he questioned the claimant with skill to the point of having her say in her testimony that her hair "looked lovely" after her services and that it "felt nice" albeit that she added "because they put all those hairdressing products in it"! What a relief when I realised that despite the ebbs and flows of the Judges summing up, he concluded that we had done everything we were expected to do in supplying a service to the claimant and that we were neither negligent nor breaching the Supply of Goods and Services Act 1982. I looked back at the girls, sitting behind me, and I mouthed 'we won'.

*Note: Our case began before the introduction of The Consumer Credit Act 2015 so was tried on the previous act - The Supply of Goods and Services Act 1982.

Shoddy Hairdressing and Poor Procedures

"Do not let counsel for the prosecution get you rattled" was the advice from our barrister as he briefed the four of us on the morning of the 19th June. "He will ask you uncomfortable questions and probe you – you must stay calm and answer the questions to the best of your knowledge and ability". And there I was – I could feel myself getting 'rattled' as the claimant's barrister asked the same questions over and over and accused me of things that I did not and would not do. Reader - have you ever been in a situation where you feel you are almost observing yourself from outside? If so you will understand how at that moment I was answering the questions, but thinking about how I could compose myself and get some control on the situation. I took a deep breath and said "I have been in the hairdressing industry for 40 years, I have been a salon owner for 28 of those, today I have 6 salons and we see between 650 and 850 clients a week,  success like that does not come from shoddy hairdressing and poor procedures". The Judge turned and looked at me intensely. The barrister was taken aback for a second, (only a second he was soon back to his questioning) and afterwards the girls said it was a defining and chilling moment in the courtroom. It is the claimant's responsibility to prove allegations against the defendant. What I have learned is it's really important to be respectful in court, however, what you say, your intention and body language are important indicators to the Judge. In simple terms you should not just sit there answering yes and no. You must get your point across in a composed and respectful way. TORT is the law used in cases of this nature against salons.

TORT Law;
Torts are wrongdoings that are done by one party against another. As a result of the wrongdoing, the injured person may take civil action against the other party. To simplify this, let's say while walking down the aisle of a grocery store, you slip on a banana that had fallen from a shelf. You become the plaintiff, or injured party, and the grocery store is considered the tortfeasor or defendant, the negligent party. Simply said, you would probably take civil action against the grocery store to recoup compensation for pain, suffering, medical bills and expenses incurred as a result of the fall. Three elements must be present;

- *Tortfeasor, or defendant, had a duty to act or behave in a certain way.*
- *Plaintiff must prove that the behaviour demonstrated by the tortfeasor did not conform to the duty owed to the plaintiff.*
- *The plaintiff suffered an injury or loss as a result.*
  Because torts are a civil action involving private parties, punishment does not include a fine or incarceration. The punishment for tortious acts usually involves restoring the injured party monetarily.

The allegations are in the claimant's witness statement and are backed up with expert reports. In all the cases I have seen the no-win no-fee relies on reports from trichologists and/or Doctors.

Definition of trichologist:
Trichology is the science and study of hair (from the Greek 'trikhos' meaning hair). Clinical trichology (i.e. trichology in the context of practising members of the Institute) is the diagnosis and treatment of diseases and disorders of the hair and scalp.

In our case the claimant had a trichologists report and a Dr's report. It then became our task to refute the claims made by the claimant supported by the reports. In summary:

- We did not use a reliable skin test method.
- Stylists were untrained and inexperienced and were not properly supervised.
- Bleach was processed under heat and for too long with higher than necessary peroxide.
- No testing to assess tolerance to the procedure or colour achievability.
- Foil was used with the bleach and caused damage.
- Lengthy period of thermal styling with a high temperature appliance.

I understand readers do not know the full details of the case and I cannot publish everything, but I have no doubt there are some details above that may surprise you. They certainly surprised us when we received the allegations – not least of all because some of the claims were simply not true (see more in Chapter 4 – DIRTY TRICKS). Suffice to say that we did skin test, the three stylists involved have collectively over 30 years of experience, the least experienced having 8 years of experience, we would NEVER process bleach under heat and ALWAYS follow manufacturers guidelines, we took strands of the clients hair and tested her hair with the actual service before the service was carried out, foil was not used with the bleach and straighteners were never used on the clients hair.

Here is the important part of this chapter, how did we prove that we are not guilty of shoddy hairdressing and poor procedures? Among the following pages are three documents we use in our salons that were imperative in the evidence. They proved that comprehensive consultations were carried out, skin testing was carried out and that a extensive method of work was completed and followed. We also supplied certificates of the stylist qualifications, photos of the claimants hair taken during and after the service, the strand tests taken from the client before the service was carried out, excerpts from hairdressing textbooks and  manufacturers instructions for all products used. All this formed the 26 pages of evidence we put forward in our defence as well as witness testimonies and other documents we produced along the way to defend the allegations against us. I mentioned in chapter 1 about precedent set, and whilst as an industry we can be relieved that Feathers have proved justice can be done in unfounded claims of negligence, my crusade is to help hairdressers and salon owners understand how to document policies and procedures in an effective way.

Feathers

Dedicated to hair.

CHEMICAL CONSULTATION SHEET

Client Name: _____

Address: _____

Telephone Number: _____

1. Have you had a perm/straightening or colour at home or in a salon in the last six months?
   YES/NO
2. Please specify the products you use at home.
   Shampoo:
   Conditioner:
   Styling products:
3. Have you had any surgery or medication within the last six months?
   YES/ NO
4. Are you pregnant or do you have an infant under the age of 8 months?
   YES /NO
5. Do you swim on a regular basis?
   YES/NO
6. Have you ever had an allergic reaction to cosmetics or a chemical hair service?
   YES/ NO
7. Do you suffer from eczema, dermatitis or psoriasis on your scalp or face?
   YES/ NO
8. Have you ever used a colour restorer of any kind? (Sun in/No More Gray etc.)
   YES/ NO
9. Have you had a temporary or permanent tattoo?
   YES/NO
10. I have completed a skin test 48 hours before this appointment and I have had no
reactions. I am happy to have colour applied to my hair and scalp.
   YES/NO

*I understand and acknowledge that a permanent hair colour application will remain in the hair
permanently, a demi-permanent hair application can last between 12 – 18 washes under normal
conditions, and a semi-permanent/temporary hair colour application lasts until the colour is removed
from the hair by repeated shampooing.*
*I understand that all the above is correct to the best of my knowledge and understand any
Incorrect information I give may affect my chemical service.*

Client Signature: _____

Stylist Signature: _____

Date: _____

Feathers

Technical Sheet

Date _____
Name _____
Service: Color ◯   Mechés/Highlift ◯   Tone on tone ◯
            Bleach ◯   SOS HCR ◯   Tone/ reflex ◯

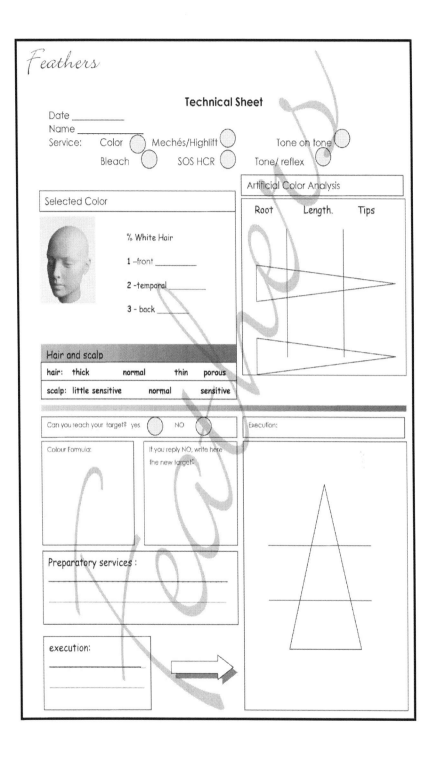

Selected Color _____

% White Hair

1 –front _____

2 –temporal _____

3 – back _____

Hair and scalp

hair:	thick	normal	thin	porous
scalp:	little sensitive	normal		sensitive

Artificial Color Analysis

Root   Length.   Tips

Can you reach your target? yes ◯   NO ◯

Colour Formula:

If you reply NO, write here the new target:

Execution:

Preparatory services :
_____
_____

execution:
_____
_____

Feathers

25 years of beautiful hair.

SKIN TESTING RECORD SHEET

Name: _____

Address: _____

Mobile Number: _____

Home Number: _____

Email: _____

SKIN TEST	DATE OF APP/CLIENT SIGNATURE	STAFF CHECK/DATE/SIGNATURE

Dirty Tricks

Do some research on solicitors who make a living from finding cases of 'negligence' that lead to personal injury claims against hairdressers. Google 'can I sue my hairdresser?' and note what comes up on your search. In the case brought against Feathers Colchester we knew we had done everything we could and should, and whilst there had been some question over whether or not the client got what she liked/wanted, we were not negligent. We felt we were the victims of a bogus claim. I am fortunate that I get to spend a lot of time with other salon owners and they often share with me their business challenges – I am well briefed in client complaints and accusations of negligence. I have heard about many spurious claims. The purpose of this book is to highlight how Feathers case was

presented and handled and some of the things I have learnt that will help others if they find themselves in similar situations. I never really got to the bottom of why, in the court papers the claimant's solicitor named me personally. The Claimant v's Deborah Digby-Smith - I can only surmise why they choose that tactic. I had never met the claimant, was not present at either of her appointments at the salon, did not speak to her on the telephone nor enter into any correspondence. What I can tell you - I felt personally attacked, intimidated and slightly exposed. Interestingly, the first thing the claimants barrister attacked me on was the fact I had not been present at any of his clients appointments so how could I be sure the evidence in my statement was true. I retorted "I did an investigation into the claims"- He replied by asking where were the notes of my investigation. I paused for a moment to think - was I supposed to have made notes? I composed myself "the result of my investigation is the collection of documents and testimonies that make up the evidence in the bundle" in the back of my mind I was thinking - I am giving testimony because you named me personally on the papers. On reflection I am glad this happened. Had they named the business, I may not have been called to give evidence. The girls said after the case it really helped them to watch me give evidence first because they then had an example of what they could and should do. I wondered for a while how they got my name until I came to realise one of the first things the no-win no-fee solicitor will do is some research on the business - and they clearly got information from Companies House. I suspect, from the many cases I have seen and from legal conversations I have had, that when a claimant's solicitor writes the first letter they use a fairly generic list of suspected events. In our case there were ten accusations listed that alleged negligence. After some correspondence between the claimant's solicitor and the loss adjuster the claims against us focused on: -

- We did not use a reliable skin test method.

We use Colourstart for every client, every service. We provided evidence to support the reliance of Colourstart and its popular use among clients and salons. In court the claimant's barrister accused me of choosing Colourstart because it is a cheaper option than regular skin testing. The Judge ruled that Colourstart is a reliable and popular method of testing. It is a good time to mention that the client claimed she had a reaction to hair colour, and then later changed that claim to a reaction to bleach. In fact she had a Drs record that stated – *Symptoms presented; 'Red confluent blanching hot maculopapular rash on forearms' Diagnosis given; allergic disorder (XalpQ)* It is really important to note that the Judge can only make a decision based upon the evidence presented to him and medical records bear weight. I have seen often in cases, Drs notes where people have presented themselves with a red rash and the Dr has diagnosed as above. Sometimes Drs actually write 'reaction to hair colour'. Anyone who has seen an allergic reaction to colour will know this is not it! Our case was well documented on both sides with photographs - interestingly there was no photographic evidence of an allergic reaction or rash put forward as evidence. I made sure the Judge was aware of this.

- Stylists were untrained and inexperienced and were not properly supervised.

We were able to demonstrate, through certificates and ongoing training records, plus the appearance and testimony of the stylists in court that all were capable of performing services and the Judge ruled so.

- Bleach was processed under heat, for too long and with higher than necessary peroxide.

This was a tough one, the allegation was supported by the trichology report. We produced records to show the check in and check out time of the client to demonstrate how long she was in the salon and that it was not possible to get all the services completed with the alleged prolonged development time. The level of peroxide used was written on the technical sheets (method of work) – but the claimant's barrister laboured the point in his questioning. He asked the same questions over and over trying to find a gap or hesitation. (Refer to the girls' accounts in chapter two – The Winners) Our testimony was strong because we had good records of the services carried out - the barrister accused us of colluding! He put it to us that we had months to get our stories straight and that we were all telling each others story. The Judge ruled that the services were carried out with due care and attention.

- No testing to assess tolerance to the procedure or colour achievability.

We took strand tests – the service to be carried out was tolerance tested. I suspect the claimant's solicitor did not think we could produce the strands. For evidence the strands were photographed and what I am going to tell you now you may find difficult to believe because I would not have believed it myself had I not seen it with my own eyes; In court the Judge, claimant's side and defendant's side are all given a 'court bundle' which is the evidence submitted before the case so that the Judge can read up before the day and it is used as reference by all witnesses and counsel during testimony. The claimants' solicitors prepare it. The photocopy of the photo of the strands was so badly copied as to not really show any conclusive evidence as to their existence. We did have them with us on the day, but were not allowed to produce evidence not previously disclosed to the court. The Judge ruled that he believed the existence of the strands. At this point I also report that the evidence we had put forward had not been indexed properly. I believe our case is not the only one where this has/may occur. My advice would be to clearly index/mark the evidence when you send it in.

- Foil was used with the bleach and caused damage.

The experts report alleged 'foil wrapped bleaching'. Interestingly the bleach was not wrapped in foil, this was added as one of those points that I suggest are just put in the allegations as a practice so widely used as to add weight to the claimant's case. Here I paraphrase what the Judge said in his summing up on this point – 'When I go to the hairdressers, I sit in the chair and take the opportunity to just relax and be still for a while, I do not take much notice of what is going on back there (waves his hand to the back of his head) and I suggest to the claimant that she could not be sure of what the hairdressers were doing during her service'.

- Lengthy period of thermal styling with a high temperature appliance.

This point was defended so passionately by Kim Watson who told the court, "I am a professional hairdresser, I know how to blow dry long hair straight – even if it is curly". Another practice so widely used it is assumed it is carried out? Salon owners and hairdressers could learn a lot about the standards expected from a professional hairdresser in this setting. Photos defended us on this point, and our barrister was so skillful  in getting the Judge to see that the allegations were unfounded. It was clear in the pictures taken in the salon that the hair had not been flat ironed as claimed.

Our case went on for two years and four months, there were long periods of silence in between (a couple of times we thought maybe the solicitors had dropped the case in light of the weight of evidence) – what I have learned is that this is a tactic used in the hope that stylists will leave the salon and therefore the witnesses disappear and along with them valuable witness testimony. And finally, you may remember Irma's account of being questioned in court – 'For a second I felt like I was in a murder case'. The performance of the witnesses in court cannot be underestimated. Here are a couple of examples of what happened to us in the courtroom: -

It seemed that if ones testimony were good and truly supporting your case, you would be cut short – butting in and asking another question was the tactic they used. It happened to me, I was cut short on a question by the barrister asking me a new, 2nd question. I was determined to answer the 1st question in full; I felt it was a really good point for our defense. I tried a couple of times but the claimant's barrister kept interrupting me, 'I am not interested in that, answer my question' he said. 'But I have not finished answering the 1st question' I said. 'Just answer the question' he said – I turned to the Judge 'Sir, if I may be allowed to finish answering the 1st question, I will happily answer the 2nd '. The Judge said 'Mrs Digby-Smith is allowed to answer the 1st question'. You have to be determined when in the courtroom with a barrister.

Those of you who have had the privilege to be in a class delivered by Brittany know her immense technical knowledge. When the claimant's barrister asked Brittany a question she answered it in FULL. I joked afterwards with the girls that it was like he asked Brittany the time and she told him how to build a watch. He was getting frustrated at her full and long answers and asked her to answer simply, she carried on answering in full and technically, she wanted the Judge to fully understand hairdressing procedures. The barrister turned to the Judge, 'Sir, please direct Mrs Newby to answer with simple answers, yes and no wherever possible'. The Judge turned to Brittany, 'continue as you are Mrs Newby, I am finding your testimony very helpful in understanding the case'.

Professional Talent and Knowledge

I believe that every cloud has a silver lining, and I do not think it is a coincidence that Kim and Irma, the two stylists involved in the case have developed into two of the highest performers in Feathers Salon Group. They have learned so much from this experience that is more to do with delivering services to customers than actually carrying out the task of  hairdressing. Let me explain - they had both done an excellent job in carrying out the service, following procedures and record keeping. That is why the case was won. But what they have learned beyond this is how to manage a clients expectations and demands. Hairdressing is perceived as

 being a simple trade to learn and deliver, but the truth could not be further from that. Hairdressing today is extremely complex, products are developing all the time with new science and technology, clients are demanding (and rightly so – when I am spending my hard earned money I am demanding too) and fashion dictates style that pushes hair (and the hairdresser) to the limit.

What is essential in our industry is ongoing education that helps the hairdresser understand what they are doing and WHY. (Even the most

advanced hairdressers). There is a specific reason that, as a hairdresser, I choose to do business with independent companies. I need to know not just the what but the WHY. And when I ask questions I need informed answers – not a fob off. The challenge our industry has to rise to is how to TEACH essential information from the point of inception (scientist or chemist), how to have hairdressers LEARN and understand how that applies in hairdressing services, and that it is their LEGAL RESPONSIBILITY and DUTY OF CARE to deliver and maintain standards. Knowing and not doing is worse than not knowing. I know hairdressers who can recite verbatim the system of delivering customer service in their salon (8 steps, 5 steps, 6 of something – all leading to the same end result – great hairdressing with home care recommendation) but they fail in their duty to deliver consistently to the clients. They mistakenly believe it is a choice whether to do or not! They would never fail to deliver again if they had to defend in a court of law the breaking off of hair after a hairdressing service they performed. (Hopefully they never have to). I know a case of a salon being sued for hair breakage after a bleaching service. The clients homecare is unknown - social media points towards home colouring over the bleach service, it would appear the client uses straighteners on her hair every day. Yet the bleaching service is being blamed for causing the breakage and the salon accused of negligence. I have been contacted by lots of people as a result of this win in court - this has given me the opportunity to collate case studies our industry can learn from. See chapters 6-13. Reader – I hope you are not reading this and saying to yourself 'this would never happen in my salon' – from the evidence I have – I believe it can happen to anyone. The question you should be asking yourself is – 'if this happened in my salon, how would we defend ourselves by proving we had carried out the services with due care and attention?' Go back to chapter three and review the documents Feathers used which formed an important part of the evidence. A consumer made contact with me after she received a straightening service that burnt her scalp and broke her hair off from the root at the crown leaving a bald patch the size of a skull cap. I was amazed to learn that she paid £50 for the service in a salon. The photos were shocking, she clearly has a case for a claim. It makes me sad to hear of this situation for everyone concerned - I am not judging - merely pointing out the need for more education in salons. A stylist told me of a client who called her for advice after her hair turned green from swimming. The stylist advised the client to use ketchup to neutralize the green. I am left wondering how the client will isolate the green from the blonde and once the hairdresser has given her advice what liability there may be?

Should you find your salon accused of negligence, you would be trying to counter the claims made by experts (trichologist/Doctor) who will be making reference to manufacturers instructions and industry standards. What methods are you using for strand testing, skin testing, incompatibility testing and assessing tolerance to planned services? More information on this in chapter 15.

Case Study One

Beverley Bates

Business is a roller coaster ride

Being a business owner and employer is certainly a big test of your metal. As we all know, it can be a roller coaster ride, the highs are thrilling and the dips can be exhausting. The lessons are just as much in the failures and challenges as they are in the good experiences. Just when you think you have seen it all, an unexpected drama can hit you and if your working practices and systems are not top notch there can be trouble ahead. I give huge thanks to Debbie Digby for many light bulb moments.

Here is my story:-

Rewind 18 years ago when running our business was so different. You would open the salon door and clients would fall in, it was way easier then in comparison to today. A busy and experienced hair extension salon, we decided to change our brand to Racoon. As part of our opening package we had a training day with a hands on workshop with a model. The trainer came to the salon to select the model and took the model through a well-documented consultation. It was stressed to the model that the particular hair type being used for the extensions needed to be maintained by drying with a hairdryer after washing and not to be left to air dry as this could cause tangling. Training day arrived and I, my senior stylist and the trainer all carried out the service and the model was very happy. The service was carried out at a discounted rate and included the first wash and blow dry in the salon to check the maintenance and quality were good. First salon visit went well and the model was happy.

Home Maintenance

Week two we received a phone call to say the model was not happy with the extensions; they were matting and starting to look a mess. The model came in for a check with me and I asked a series of careful questions (which I documented) – one of the questions was 'how have you been washing and styling your hair?' her reply 'the weather has been so nice I have been sitting in the sun to let it dry'. If I had asked 'have you been blow drying your hair as directed'? I suspect she would have replied yes – so I am so pleased I asked the questions in the way I did. She had been sent home

with a maintenance brochure but it appeared she was ignoring the advice we had given her and the instructions in the brochure. I asked the model to sign the documented questions and answers and suggested an action plan moving forward. If we were to cut 2 inches from the length of the hair the hair extensions could be salvaged, and I reinforced the importance of the maintenance, in particular drying with a hairdryer. I assured her it would look fabulous once again.

Extensions are a commitment

This is where it started to nosedive – the mood changed and the model was clearly upset, she said she had not paid all this money to have her hair cut shorter. Knowing that this was not going to end well, I told the model that I would be in touch with Racoon for advice and I would be back in touch immediately. The model left the salon feeling less upset. I contacted Racoon who sent the trainer to the models house, she reported that indeed the matting was caused by the home maintenance and confirmed that with a trim and better homecare the situation would rectify. Racoon reported to me that the model seemed OK with the outcome. I phoned the model to follow up and she said she was not happy and agreed to come to the salon to meet with me. I asked Racoon if we could replace some or all of the hair for a fresh start – they agreed to this. When I met with the model she would not agree to this and still said she wanted her money back. I explained this was not an option and she got really angry. I pointed out that her lack of home maintenance had caused the problems, but as a gesture of goodwill we would replace the hair. She was adamant we had not made the home maintenance clear and she wanted her money back or else. As the conversation was getting heated I suggested we should meet again the following day to continue the discussion.

I sensed a bigger problem

I immediately phoned the insurance company and put them in touch with Racoon. The next day the model came in with her husband. Her hair extensions were in a bag, she had them taken out by a competitor who had told her they were poor quality and we had done a poor job. She told me if she did not get her money back AND compensation there and then, there was going to be trouble. I again went over the sequence of events and expressed that a refund was not an option (this was hard to stand up to – part of me wanted to cave in and get rid of the aggravation but knowing we had

done nothing wrong I was angry and wanted to do the right thing). The conversation became abusive and I asked her and her husband to leave. When I left the salon that evening the two of them were waiting outside and shouted abuse. I ignored them and walked passed. I received a phone call from the model to say she was starting a petition to get me closed down. She was going to sue me for personal injury as this had affected her scalp and caused her emotional distress. I put it in the hands of the insurers. Unbelievably they informed me they wanted to pay out. Racoon stepped in to support me and we were both adamant that this should not be the case. The owner of Racoon, Peter Holloway was with me every step of the way.

Standing up for what is right

We had to find a solicitor to represent me. It would have been the easy option to try and hide the saga from our clients, but the reality was we were being bad mouthed and our reputation that we had worked so hard for was being jeopardised. If I have done something wrong, and we all make mistakes from time to time, I am the first to put my hands up and say sorry, but if someone is trying to do me over, I am going to stand up for what is right. I decided to tell everyone the story, in an adult and factual way. Never underestimate the power of your network; it will always come good for you. One of my clients was a solicitor and she offered her services free of charge! It took 10 agonizing months to get to court; the continuing abuse from the model, the worry and the shame of being talked about was just horrible at the time. Doing all this without the insurance behind me was a concern and I was scared about receiving a huge bill. The day before we went to court the model said she would settle for £3000. We politely declined her offer.

Justice

On court day I was terrified but with a fire in my belly and the right support by my side it wasn't as bad as I thought. It is true the anticipation can be worse than reality. The judge found her guilty of trying to extract monies. In the Judges words - our complaints procedure was watertight and our standards of professionalism were clearly proven. The flowers and well wishes from clients were overwhelming.

What did I learn?

Without documenting every conversation and having good working practices this model would have won. We found out after the incident that this was a regular activity for her. She had succeeded with insurance claims previously. It would appear the insurers prefer to pay out and put up our premiums to cover the costs. I learned that not only do the creative services that we offer have to be a high standard; we have to operate as if every client may potentially sue us. So long as we have the wellbeing of the client as paramount and can prove our intention and professionalism, everything will be OK. If a ruthless client tries to do us over, we can defend ourselves. Our learning must never stop, the hair and fashion industry is fast paced and with laws and regulations changing all the time it is important to stay current and informed.

Debbie's comments

Documentation

Those involved had done a really good job of documenting the services and giving the homecare in the form of a take home leaflet.

'The trainer came to the salon to select the model and took the model through a well-documented consultation.'

Note when Beverley asked questions they were open questions which required the model to give a full answer in her own words which meant Beverly got more information – the questions were not loaded with the assumption of the expected answer.

'how have you been washing and styling your hair?' her reply 'the weather has been so nice I have been sitting in the sun to let it dry'. If I had asked 'have you been blow drying your hair as directed'? I suspect she would have replied yes – so I am so pleased I asked the questions in the way I did.'

Another example of a loaded question could be 'Are you shampooing with a professional shampoo'? When asked this question a client may answer yes, but when asked which brand may not be able to be specific.

Refunds and apologies

There are some common misconceptions about giving money back that are worth noting;
Beverley wrote -

'When I met with the model she would not agree to this and still said she wanted her money back. I explained this was not an option and she got really angry. I pointed out that her lack of home maintenance had caused the problems, but as a gesture of goodwill we would replace the hair.'

The following day when they met it escalated –

'Her hair extensions were in a bag, she had them taken out by a competitor who had told her they were poor quality and we had done a poor job. She told me if she did not get her money back AND compensation there and then, there was going to be trouble.'

If you issue an apology, offer a service or to refund a clients money after a service this is not an inference of guilt or fault. Section 2 of the Compensation Act 2006 is unequivocal. "An apology, an offer of treatment or other redress, shall not of itself amount to an admission of negligence or breach of statutory duty." In fact an early and genuine apology can do much good at no cost. If you are going to compensate a client with a refund or other monies it may be wise to make your offer - in Full and Final Settlement - if that is what you intend. If this is the case you should consider taking a little legal advice. It does not have to cost much to get legal advice in this case and may prove invaluable. It is important to understand that whilst giving money back for a haircut a client is not happy with may satisfy your obligation under the Consumer Rights Act 2015, if a client has suffered personal injury, (this could be damage to the scalp or hair) a Full and Final Settlement offer may not be appropriate.

Insurance company payout

'(this was hard to stand up to – part of me wanted to cave in and get rid of the aggravation but knowing we had done nothing wrong I was angry and wanted to do the right thing)'

said Beverley about the experience.

'I put it in the hands of the insurers. Unbelievably they informed me they wanted to pay out.'

It is common for insurers to pay out because, unbelievably, this is often the cheaper and easier option. The other problem for cases in the hairdressing industry is the lack of evidence. In a conversation with a commercial solicitor who defends salons he summed this problem up simply; I asked "why is the hairdressing industry receiving so much attention from no-win no-fee companies?" – his reply, "unfortunately Debbie, most salons are cannon fodder for these solicitors." He was referring to the ease with which claims can be made that cannot be defended through lack of tangible documentation. Note in Chapter 2 where I refer to QOCS 'Qualified one-way costs shifting' and consider also the cost of the solicitors and if it goes to court – the cost of a barrister.

Complaints procedure

'our complaints procedure was watertight and our standards of professionalism were clearly proven'

Make sure you have a documented procedure that is published, for example on your website, and that it complies with the Consumer Rights Act 2016. Ensure your team carryout your policy and that you make reference to your 'complaints procedure' or 'guarantee of satisfaction' in any correspondence.

Accountable

'I learned that not only do the creative services that we offer have to be a high standard; we have to operate as if every client may potentially sue us.'

I refer back to Chapter 1 – Hair Industry Regulation? We have it....... Yes we are being held accountable and when tested, many salons and stylists are failing in their duty under the Consumer Rights Act (to carry out services of a satisfactory quality and as described and fit for purpose and last a reasonable length of time) or are not able to produce proof that defends any accusations.

Case Study Two

Anonymous

Professional standards

Throughout my career I have found that skin testing is very lenient in salons. When I opened my own salon, I wanted it to be professional. I thought "What can I do to make the salon have its own unique selling point?" and from that I decided that our trademark would be a strong consultation before the appointment. This would enable us to provide the best possible service as it gave us an opportunity to assess the type, structure and condition of the hair and allow us to skin test the client at the same time. This is not something we can easily do on the phone. We often get clients who do not want a consultation – they see it as too much bother, however what we have found is that clients who want a consultation service are the best kind of clients to have, as it tells us they care enough about their own

hair. It helps ensure our stylists have enough time booked out to complete the service, rather than only having an hour booked when the client has hair down to their ankles and we need triple the amount of time. As a busy salon, a consultation before the appointment helps our stylists stay well prepared and our clients are happy as we can apply a skin test ready for the

appointment. We use a sophisticated booking system that stores colour notes and other information with a timestamp, meaning we can check the history, date and time of previous notes, skin tests and any other recorded information. I never considered that feature would prove so vital with our insurance.

Allergies

Now, the first time we ever had to deal with the possibility of a client suing us was when a client arrived for a consultation and announced she was allergic to PPD. As we are hair extension specialists, we carried out a colour match during the consultation. She previously had highlights carried out by a mobile hairdresser and realised she had an allergy to PPD after having a henna tattoo on holiday. Following manufacturer's instructions, we skin tested the client with two ranges of colour in the shades we would be using. A traditional line and a PPD free line. During the consultation, we were vigilant in asking questions to ascertain if the client had an irritation or reaction before proceeding with the colour service. She told us it was an irritation after we explained the difference. We booked the client in and waited for her appointment, asking her to let us know of any problems with the test. She arrived for her appointment stating she had itchiness from one test, which was the traditional line, but the PPD free line was fine. We proceeded to apply a root tint using the PPD free colour and throughout the

process I asked "How does the product feel? Is it tingling? Does it feel warm?" to which she said "No – it is the best a hair dye has ever felt and one time I was hospitalised!" I thought to myself "Hospitalised?!" During the consultation when we asked the client about any previous reactions or irritations, she said "redness and itchiness" now she tells me she was hospitalised…I  immediately rinsed the colour off, advised her to take antihistamines and to consult a doctor if the condition worsened. I felt confident about the outcome as I suffer from irritation to tint, so knowing the PPD free formula is great on my own hair and scalp, I felt all would be OK. The client told me she was going on holiday the next day and was going for brow and nail treatments to finish off the pamper day.

See you in Court

Three days later I received the dreaded email, with a subject written like a newspaper headline! "Help {Salon Name} Customer Hospitalised" I couldn't swallow properly and instantly panicked! "What had happened?" I asked myself. The email asked what products were used, for the doctor. I took a screenshot of the notes and sent them over. I was fully compliant as I didn't want anything bad to happen. I was extremely empathetic, I passed on my sadness and couldn't imagine what they were going through! The client's mother sent pictures through and I completely broke down! I was informed she went on holiday with her sister and was flown home in an emergency and hospitalised. When I received a picture of her face she was unrecognisable! Her face was five times the normal size, it was so scary. I felt dreadful! I messaged a few times to see if she was OK and checked back in a few days later. That is when her mother became nasty. The client had come to the salon for a new look, on recommendation from a family where all the females visit us. She even sent an email on the same day of her appointment to say how happy she was and how amazing her hair looked, so I couldn't understand why the tone had changed. The client's mother said "My daughter could have died because of your salon!" I could not understand where these accusations were coming from, I was on edge for days – I couldn't eat or sleep. Nothing like this had happened in my career and the skin test didn't show any signs of irritation or reaction. I just couldn't fathom what went wrong. Her mother said she was too upset to talk to me and "see you in court".

Social Media

When the client was discharged from hospital, a lengthy Facebook post with pictures surfaced. In the post, it mentioned they were taking our salon to court and the horrific pictures were attached. They did not name the salon, however they denied she had a skin test and said they didn't want anyone else to go through what she had…I couldn't grasp it myself and thought "Do they not know what we had talked about? Do they not understand  that the colour we applied to her skin was a test?" Another stylist and I had physically seen her in person for the consultation so I wondered "Why are they denying it now?" It was from that moment alarm bells were ringing. I thought "Could the skin test have triggered something?" but soon realised it could not have been that as her actual appointment was a week after the skin test. At that point I remembered her saying she was going for a brow treatment that same day, immediately after her hair appointment. Now, I know from experience that I cannot have a brow tint as I am allergic to the key ingredient in the tint, and the irritation is much more severe than hair colour due to an increased risk of contact with the skin. Previously my skin has swollen, blistered and wept, therefore I know to stay well away. Brow tints contain PPD and are strong in formulation. I did some research on Facebook and found where she had her brows tinted. Lo and behold she was tagged in a picture with very obvious newly dyed brows. It is the one thing my husband commented on when I showed him the picture. He said "Her brows are very dark aren't they". It appeared it was her friend that had done them, so she obviously didn't want to admit the brow tint could have been the cause of her severe reaction, instead slanderous claims were made against my business with the hope of an insurance pay-out. The whole experience left me feeling numb, several discussions with lawyers appointed by the insurance company and many

phone calls later, I was interviewed and asked to submit all of my evidence.

Saving grace

I strongly believe my saving grace was that I carried out a skin test and the booking system clearly showed the date of the skin test, proving I followed manufacturer's instructions. I will never know what caused the irritation, but I know as a salon we did the right thing, and it is such a shame that we are one of the very few salons who insist on patch testing every client and even we were almost sued despite the precautions we take. I was able to prove that we skin test every client as we regularly offer last minute appointments on our Facebook page and months before a client had posted "Oh I know you're really insistent on patch testing, but can I have this appointment please as I haven't got time for a skin test and want the colour done today?". We replied "Unfortunately, all clients need an up to date skin test at our salon in order to carry out a colour service." I don't feel we lose any business by skin testing and I will most certainly continue to do it. If a new stylist asks "Why?" (as their previous salon may not have bothered to skin test), I explain we want the best clientele. If they are willing to come in for a consultation, colour match and skin test, it often indicates they want the best for their hair and will look after it. If they don't, chances are they are just there for a short-term fix and not the long-lasting clientele we are looking for. We are still a very busy and successful salon, so this experience has in no way hindered our business. I am so glad I had proof as the case went on for what felt like years. I hope all stylists are responsible when colouring and do not end up in a horrific situation where they are liable for something that is so easily avoidable. I drum it into the head of every stylist I employ and I am so glad I was the stylist who dealt with this particular client, for I fear it could have knocked the confidence of a less experienced stylist. I know companies out there exist to get rich quick from 'no win no fee' cases, however if you have the proof to discredit any claim of negligence, at least then it voids these companies profiting from hardworking salons. I feel the client should have taken personal responsibility for hair colouring and been truthful from the beginning. I hope now she will stay away from colouring.

Debbie's comments

Choose your clients

I love the way this salon know who they want as clients.

'However what we have found is that clients who want a consultation service are the best kind of clients to have, as it tells us they care enough about their own hair'

I also admire their policy of planning complex services in advance so they may book out the right amount of time for a service and manage client's expectations.

'It helps ensure our stylists have enough time booked out to complete the service, rather than only having an hour booked when the client has hair down to their ankles and we need triple the amount of time. As a busy salon, a consultation before the appointment helps our stylists stay well prepared'

In my opinion, strand testing and in depth consultations are the way forward when dealing with clients with high expectations for complex services. We may joke about clients that want to go from box dye black to blonde in two hours and under £100, and I do think we are seeing expectations becoming more realistic, but there are still many situations that are not properly managed and planned and these are the situations that will lead salons and stylists into trouble.

Allergy alert

We are presented with more and more people with allergies and sensitivities.

'She realised she had an allergy to PPD after having a henna tattoo on holiday.'

It is important that hairstylists become experts in understanding what factors are contributing to allergies and reactions, and the difference in a reaction, irritation and sensitivity. I know clients who have presented themselves as allergic to PPD, and when questioned have discovered this from tests at a sensitivity clinic. This is not a reason to not proceed with a service if you have a PPD free colour and the client passes a skin test. There are also many examples of clients who have not completely disclosed all the information so desperate are they to have their hair coloured. This is what makes documented consultation so important.

"How does the product feel? Is it tingling? Does it feel warm?" to which she said, "No – it is the best a hair dye has ever felt and one time I was hospitalised!" I thought to myself "Hospitalised?!" During the consultation when we asked the client about any previous reactions or irritations, she said "redness and itchiness" now she tells me she was hospitalised...'

Do some research on the internet and read the accounts from people that have suffered hair color reactions. I am aware of many instances where women have been hospitalised with a hair colour reaction, advised to never colour their hair again, but still go in search of a solution to colouring their hair. If you read carefully the manufacturers instructions you are cautioned – do not use this product if you have ever experienced any reaction after colouring your hair. This is because once a client has experienced a reaction to hair colour dye, the immune system 'remembers' the chemical and will launch a defense reaction the next time you are exposed to it.

'I was informed she went on holiday with her sister and was flown home in an emergency and hospitalised. When I received a picture of her face she was unrecognisable!'

The pictures in this case were shocking.

'Her face was five times the normal size it was so scary. I felt dreadful!'

But what was interesting was the swelling was prominent across the eyes. There was no swelling to the head, and from the pictures you could not see any redness or weeping of the scalp.

'At that point I remembered her saying she was going for a brow treatment that same day'

Do some research.

'A lengthy Facebook post with pictures surfaced. In the post, it mentioned they were taking our salon to court and the horrific pictures were attached. They did not name the salon, however they denied she had a skin test'

Chapter 14 addresses social media suffice to say here that the salon owner used social media to her advantage – she found evidence that the client had her brows done on the same day.

'At that point I remembered her saying she was going for a brow treatment that same day, immediately after her hair appointment.'

Why were they focusing on the hair treatment being at fault?

'It appeared it was her friend that had done them, so she obviously didn't want to admit the brow tint could have been the cause of her severe reaction, instead slanderous claims were made against my business with the hope of an insurance pay-out.'

A very good friend of mine (not in the hair industry) had a very serious court case that she won, and one of the things she shared with me after her case was if I were ever in a similar situation, 'do not assume that the solicitor will do all the work'. (Investigating, gathering evidence etc.) She advised me – 'do as much of the work yourself as you can, ' – It proved to be great advice. During the Feathers Colchester case we had three different solicitors. (I have learned that staff retention in the legal industry may be similar to that of hairdressing) With each new solicitor, I ensured that the case and evidence were intact, had I have not done, we would not have got to court. This salon owner also did a lot of the work herself.

Our obligation

'I will never know what caused the irritation, but I know as a salon we did the right thing'

We are not able to control and prevent everything, but as long as we have done all we are required to do we have done our best, and will be defendable. It is not as difficult as it may seem, follow manufacturers instructions and be informed about professional standards – up to date NVQ books are a great reference in the salon. Also attend education events held by manufacturers and distributors. DO NOT rely on what you see and read on social media; I shudder at some of the things I see on social media – beware fake news.

Protect your business

'I fear it could have knocked the confidence of a less experienced stylist.'

I have seen many hairstylists confidence knocked by legal cases, complaints and social media reviews posts. My very own Irma Majauskaite reports in chapter 2 how our case stopped her from teaching others and I know stylists who have left our profession to escape the pressure and stress of such instances. Invest resource to ensure that everyone in your business is well trained and informed. Technology and fashion changes all the time so ongoing CPD (Continuing Professional Development) for hairdressers is imperative. Uphold the standards in your salon; do not allow shortcuts or services that are not well planned. Be prepared to let some clients go to another salon if they do not want to take your advice or pay your prices. One of my salons had a client who walked out of a consultation because she felt the stylist's advice was because she simply wanted to make more money from the client. The manager reiterated the stylists' advice and the client angrily stormed out of the salon. She later left a 1* review for us on social media. Whilst I wish the outcome were a satisfied client, I completely respect the stylist and managers' knowledge and decision.

'I feel the client should have taken personal responsibility for hair colouring and been truthful from the beginning'

A client does have responsibility to be truthful, but this does not relinquish a hairdressers' responsibility to act professionally. In legal cases where both parties are somewhat in the wrong, contributory negligence can reduce a claim, there is more about this in Chapter 8.

Finally

The client denied that she had her brows done; social media evidence was put forward to support the salon owners' belief that she had them done. The salon owner insisted the insurance company should not pay out whilst she gathered more evidence and put forward questions to be answered by the client. It is important to remember that the insurance company and solicitors working on your behalf will have little knowledge of hairdressing products and processes, but remember the evidence and questions you put forward must be backed by independent verification.

Case Study Three

Kimberley LeVine

Perm damage

Our client, Mrs Smith enlisted a no-win no-fee solicitor and they wrote to me claiming that Mrs Smith's hair had been damaged due to a perm one of our stylists had carried out for her. In the letter it stated that Mrs Smith had been unhappy at the time of the visit as she felt the stylist had 'rushed' her and that her hair felt dry when she left. Mrs Smith did contact us a week after her visit to inform us how she felt. We invited her back in for a check up on the perm and a consultation as to how we could help her moving forward. We asked Mrs Smith to bring in all the products and tools she had at home that she was using on her hair. Mrs Smith came to us 6 days after the perm and her hair looked pretty good but it did look as if it had not been blow dried or finished very well.

Maintaining the style

Following the consultation it was clear that Mrs Smith was leaving her hair to partially dry naturally and then was using a hot brush to finish. We got Mrs Smith to show us what she was doing and gave lots of help and tips on how she could improve her ability to dry her hair smooth. Mrs Smith took on board what we said and booked in to have her roots tinted the following week. As a gesture of

goodwill, we offered a complimentary blow dry a couple of days later, to demonstrate how to smooth the hair and achieve the look she wanted. Following her colour appt. Mrs Smith was extremely happy and left the salon full of praise for her stylist. On returning from her holiday, Mrs Smith got back in touch to ask if she could book more blow dry appointments as she was struggling to manage it herself. We booked the appointments and offered the first 2 visits complimentary. On one of the occasions the salon manager called to confirm the appointment and spoke to a colleague of Mrs Smith's who said that she had gone to lunch and would pass on the message confirming the date and time.

Claims

Mrs Smith did not attend her blow dry. Instead the letter arrived from a no-win no-fee in Manchester claiming -

1. Irreversible damage to her hair.
2. No strand test carried out.
3. Staff who were not qualified were let 'loose' on Mrs Smith's hair.
4. The perm was left on too long and consequently the hair over processed.
5. Perm was not rinsed and neutralised sufficiently.
6. The incident caused so much upset and stress that she took 6 months off work, and that it ruined her holiday.
7. She was so distressed by the whole thing that she had undergone cognitive behavioural therapy for stress.
8. All this added to a total claim of £12,000.

As you would expect, we contested all of the claims. Our insurer appointed a solicitor for us and together we addressed each point raised.

1. Irreversible damage to the hair (we said categorically no to this)
2. No strand test carried out (we did and had technical notes on her technical sheet to prove this)
3. Staff who were not qualified were let 'loose' on Mrs Smith's hair. (The stylist concerned was a qualified stylist to NVQ level 3)
4. The perm was left on too long and consequently the hair over processed. (We maintained that a timer had been used and therefore was not on too long)

5. Perm was not rinsed and neutralised sufficiently. (Again, stressed that we had used a timer)
6. The incident caused so much upset and stress that she took 6 months off work, and that it ruined her holiday. (I had dates to show when I had called and spoken to her at work which clashed with dates she was supposedly off)
7. The incident caused so much upset and stress that she took 6 months off work, and that it ruined her holiday.
8. All this added to a total claim of £12,000

Court appearance

During the court hearing a trichologist made a mockery of the whole thing. He made comments about 'how pretty' the hairdressers were and that he was sorry to have to go against them like this! He said that all perm processes damage the hair and used a small red conventional perm rod to demonstrate how hair is wrapped around overlapping and therefore the water and neutraliser could not have penetrated through to the ends. We arrived prepared. When the stylist took the stand, she had a Molton Brown sponge twister as this is what was used, not the red conventional roller. The stylist demonstrated how the hair had been wound across the full length of the roller to allow even penetration and to prevent the hair being overlapped as it was wound.

Regarding the strand test, Mrs Smith said that there had been no hair taken for a 'strand test'. The stylist agreed, but added that the hair did not need to be removed and that it was a process carried out without her realising. When the timing issue was raised, we had check in and check out times to show that she had not been in the salon any longer than she should have been.

The Judge took 30 minutes to make his decision.

1. Irreversible damage to her hair THIS WAS UPHELD
2. Did not carry out strand test. JUDGE DISPUTED THIS
3. That we let staff that were not qualified 'loose' on Mrs Smith's hair. JUDGE DISPUTED THIS
4. That we left the perm on and consequently it over processed. JUDGE DISPUTED THIS
5. That we did not rinse and neutralise sufficiently. JUDGE DISPUTED THIS

6. That we caused her so much upset and stress that she took 6 months off work, and that it ruined her holiday. JUDGE DISPUTED THIS

7. The solicitor also said that that she was so distressed by the whole thing that she had undergone cognitive behavioural therapy for stress.

8. All this added to a total claim of £12,000. JUDGE SAID £12K WAS FAR TOO MUCH AND AWARDED HER £1000.

The insurance company supported us through this claim so they paid the costs of the defence and the court.

Debbie's comments

'We asked Mrs Smith to bring in all the products and tools she had at home that she was using on her hair.'

A common problem with post service complaints is that the client cannot or will not maintain her hair and style. This is a common problem nowadays with the fashion pastel, silver and direct colours. Clients do not always appreciate the upkeep of their chosen look. It is important that stylists fully inform the client of the upkeep needed and get the clients agreement for the time and money investment. I know of a couple of salons that price the home care into the price of the service because of the importance of the maintenance of the clients new hair extensions or the upkeep of the pastel lilac toner. In Mrs Smith's case she clearly had her own idea of how she thought she could style her hair and get the same result as the stylist. I can appreciate why Kimberley pushed the insurance company to defend the case, it appears they had done nothing wrong with the service, and supported the client when she was having trouble styling her hair. A difficult dilemma in these cases is where to draw the line with support. I know of a case where the client was supported by the salon for over a year with complimentary hairdressing. When the salon tried to bring the support to a polite close, the client turned to a no-win no-fee. This case is 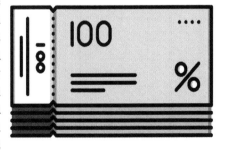 ongoing, and the insurance company are defending the case. It is important to note that a client has three years with which to bring a claim.

Generic claims

'During the court hearing a trichologist made a mockery of the whole thing.'

The part a trichologist plays in legal cases against hairdressers is documented in chapter 3. They are the specialists relied upon in court to make a report to help the Judge understand the complexity of a case. Many are hairdressers, but they may not have practiced for years. I have seen some trichology reports that are not accurate because the information in the report has not taken into account technological advances in products or practices. I want to note not all trichologists work against hairdressers. I have seen a case recently where a salon was accused of not skin testing before a bleach service. A trichologist made a report in defense of the hairdresser to demonstrate that a skin test is not an appropriate test for a bleaching service. A hairdresser will understand that anyone and everyone will have itching and redness if bleach touches the skin. What I will say on this point; many hairdressers do not apply bleach with the correct method – particularly when bleaching roots. Kimberley's case demonstrates my points made in chapter 4 regarding the authenticity of the information and the generic manner in which accusations can be made. The emphasis then becomes on the defendant to prove the allegations are not true or accurate.

Reduced award

'All this added to a total claim of £12,000. JUDGE SAID £12K WAS FAR TOO MUCH AND AWARDED HER £1000.'

It is possible for a Judge to apply a reduction in damages due to contributors negligence, we do not know if this is why the judge lowered the award to Mrs Smith, but it could be an interesting point in some future cases.

The costs

'The insurance company supported us through this claim so they paid the costs of the defence and the court.'

The main point of this book is right here. Forewarned is Forearmed. If a client suffers injury or wrongdoing whilst in someone else's care – example whilst in a salon receiving a treatment – it is right that the client should receive compensation for losses and pain and suffering. It has been said already in this book that if one is at fault one is happy to raise their hands and take responsibility. We pay for insurance, because things can go wrong despite every precaution being taken. But what we have today is the claims industry seeking opportunity in sloppy hairdressing practices and poorly informed hairdressers. I read many forums and threads on social media where hairdressers are helping each other and giving advice - I applause the sentiment of the intention. However, often I see things written that are just not correct. I saw a comment recently where a hairdresser rejected the notion of skin testing with the rational that she had been hairdressing 30 years and is yet to see a client have an allergy to hair colour. She is completely missing the point and is clearly not engaged in the industry. What is concerning is that other hairdressers are making decisions based on her comment.

Case Study Four

Anonymous

Competition work

The hair was being done free of charge and YD was happy to be a model for a photo shoot. She was excited about the possibility of getting through to a competition. The stylist had been friendly with YD out of work since asking her to be a model. The stylist did her hair on a Sunday when the salon was closed to ensure all effort went in without any distraction.

Service one

Virgin hair (except very ends)⬜ lightened with bleach. Processed for 35 minutes. Once rinsed and dried bleach + 10 volume peroxide put on some ends where the hair needed lifting more. Left for 15-20 minutes development time. The stylist toned after and throughout the process a bond repairer was used to protect the hair. The result was great. The hair felt strong and YD and stylist were very happy. We gave the client products to use at home. Protein based is what we recommend for lightened hair and a leave in treatment.

Service two

Roots lightened with bleach. Timer set for 30 minutes. Bleach +10 volume applied to midshaft and ends for the last 15-20 minutes as colour had got slightly yellow over the 11 weeks. A bond repairer was used exactly like the previous service. The stylist checked the hair throughout, stretching strands to check colour and strength. The stylist rinsed the hair a couple of minutes after the 30 minutes development as she was checking it had lifted to the correct colour. Our bleach can be left on the scalp for 50 minutes so it wasn't over processed.

Breakage

When the water hit the hair at the basin the hair began to break at the point where the freshly coloured hair met the already coloured hair. All the regrowth was still attached and very strong but the majority of the length broke away. The hair that came away was strong and not behaving like over processed hair. Her scalp was healthy on the day and day after. We also met her two days later and the scalp still looked well.

What was different?

This service is done in our salon on a weekly basis with the same products and we get perfect results every time. We have been open for 6.5

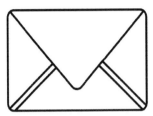

years with no problems previously. I kept some of the hair and testing it, it feels strong and not like over processed hair. ⏎I have sent the hair away to a trichologist, recommended to me by the National Hairdressing Federation in hope of finding out exactly what has happened. He is writing a report for me.

Moving forward

The stylist worked with the client to choose a short style as there was slightly more hair around the face. The colour of the bleach needed toning so they agreed to tone the roots. The stylist wanted to get the best possible style in the situation and wanted to cancel the competition that was on the following day. YD was strong in saying to the stylist she wanted to go ahead with it and the show must go on. Even on the morning of the competition she didn't back down and we attended.

A change in attitude

Days later, we met with YD; she wanted us to make her a financial offer. She got quite nasty and said if we didn't she would sue us. The next day YD had her hair cut in a salon nearby even shorter.

Collating information

YD said she used what we gave her at home but also a baby shampoo and had previously told the stylist she used coconut oil. The stylist had told her not to use the coconut oil anymore. She has since said there is a well in her garden which could possibly cause a chemical in-balance in the water. The stylist has been hairdressing 11.5 years and is the top stylist in our salon. She is also one of our bleaching specialists, she has clients that return for the exact service YD had again and again. She is NVQ 2&3 qualified and has a list of courses and education she has achieved. No tests were carried out prior to the second application. The stylist tested the hair throughout the bleaching process without any concerns. ⬜The hair only had the services we had carried out to our knowledge, so we were confident not to strand test. If any professional hairdresser carried out a tensile strength test [pull test] I believe they would not have found any reason to not continue a second colour service on YD.

Debbie's comments

Competition work

'The hair was being done free of charge and YD was happy to be a model for a photo shoot.'

When working with house models it would be wise to have an agreement in place regarding the nature of receiving free services in return for this type of work. This does not relinquish a hairdresser from their professional duty to carry out services in a proper manner, but does ensure that you can demonstrate all parties discussed and understood the agreement.

Hairdressing on the salon premises

'The stylist had been friendly with YD out of work since asking her to be a model. The stylist did her hair on a Sunday when the salon was closed to ensure all effort went in without any distraction.'

Salon owners should be aware that if services are being carried out on your premises you could be responsible for the outcome of such services even if you are not there or the 'client' is not paying. I often hear people say 'she is a regular client' – we have plenty of evidence in these case studies that regular clients or indeed friends can sue as easily as anyone else. In my salons I insist every client, every service for skin testing, even my mother, who put the team into a tailspin when she told them she did not need a skin test because she is my mother! I telephoned her, "mother, put your skin test on please and show the stylist when you have your consultation with her."

Assumptions

'This service is done in our salon on a weekly basis with the same products and we get perfect results every time. We have been open for 6.5 years with no problems previously.'

It is easy to assume from what we see, but hair has more than one dimension. There are a lot of factors that can affect hair; well water in this case may have made a difference to the hair structure. The fact that the ends had discoloured could be evidential to this. But I think if bleach on hair reacts with metal it heats up – doesn't it? You see we have to understand there are aspects of hair that cannot be seen by the eye. We cannot always predict when mixing chemicals with the complex hair structure what the outcome will be.

Working together

'I have sent the hair away to a trichologist, recommended to me by the National Hairdressing Federation in hope of finding out exactly what has happened. He is writing a report for me.'

It makes me happy to read this. The salon owner reached out for help in the industry, NHF and a trichologist, in this case Brian Plunkett stepped in to help. It was Brian who introduced me to this salon owner so she could get as much support and advice as was possible to find. There were some compelling photos in this case, the salon owner was advised to settle this case.

Case Study Five

Anonymous

Skin test

A new client to the salon found us when she was researching PPD free colour. She told us that she was allergic to PPD but had not had a previous reaction. She lived a distance from the salon so in the first instance we sent a Colourstart test and asked her to test herself. She passed the Colourstart test so we asked her to come to the salon to be tested with the actual colour. We tested by applying colour on the inside of the arm. She completed a questionnaire and circled NO to the question *'Have you ever had an allergic reaction to cosmetics or a chemical hair service?'*

Reaction

We proceeded with the service and she was over the moon with the result. She stated she had not felt any uncomfortable sensation during the service. All seemed well until we got a call from her mother-in-law two days later to say she had been admitted to hospital with a severe allergic reaction. We were baffled. We had followed every procedure and manufacturers instruction. We contacted the colour manufacturer and Colourstart.

Everyone was showing the upmost concern. I called the client's partner that evening to find out how she was and he was really angry. He revealed to me that she had a previous reaction and assumed that we were to blame. I let him vent at that point and did not say too much for fear of incriminating the business.

No case

I took legal advice the next day and was advised that she did not have a case because she had been asked about previous reactions and had circled and signed. The next day I called her partner and told him about the form she had signed. He said he would see me in court and that they had a solicitor on the case. I waited for a letter but instead the client called out of the blue and said she wanted to talk to me about compensation. She had been off work for six weeks, suffering depression etc. I stood firm and told her that we would not be offering her any compensation. We assumed by this time that the solicitor had decided there was not a clear cut case because we had followed all procedures and she had not declared her previous reactions despite our questionnaire she had completed and signed.

Looking for solutions

I met with the client and her mother-in-law to discuss what had happened and show her mother in law the documents we had. In that meeting the client was still asking me questions about how she could cover her white hair in the future.

Debbie's comments

Colourstart

At Feathers we use Colourstart to skin test every client, every service. In our court case the use of Colourstart was accepted by the insurance company but attacked by the prosecution on the court day. There are manufacturers who advise against its use. Here is what I know. Colourstart is widely used in salons and accepted by many insurance companies as a reliable and professional alternative to the traditional industry 'blob' test. It can be conveniently applied by the client at home, is waterproof, suitable for all makes and shades of hair dye and carries £2m product liability and failure insurance keeping your client safe and giving you peace of mind. Instructions for use must be followed carefully.

Previous history

I have found it to be a common problem that the hairdresser does not have all the relevant information regarding their client's hair history. This could be because the hairdresser is not asking the right questions, the client does not know or remember the information or the relevance and/or importance of information is not fully appreciated. This makes the documented consultation an important part of a chemical service.

Different outcome

There could have been a very different story in this case had the salon not been able to demonstrate that they had given the client the opportunity to divulge her previous reaction. It is interesting that in this case it appears the client could not get a no-win no-fee to represent her. It is important for us to realise that if we have the right procedures and documentation in place we can defend our professional actions. I have seen a letter from no-win no-fee to a prospective client stating; "From what you have told me it would seem you have reasonable grounds to bring a claim for compensation against (the hairdresser) providing she has the correct insurance in place." In a recent workshop on this subject I shared the letter with the group. A salon owner exclaimed 'so I would be better off with no insurance?' – answer – depends how much your business is worth or worth to you, and if you have any money in the bank or equity in your  house! I am aware of some cases involving hairdressers with no insurance, a little like car drivers with no insurance – it can be difficult and expensive to bring a legal case. However if you have any assets - beware.

Follow manufacturers instructions

This client was searching for a solution for her allergy, possibly believing that her reaction was brand specific. I have seen from hairdressing forums on social media hairdressers who believe this also. If you read carefully the manufacturers instructions you are cautioned – do not use this product if you have ever experienced any reaction after colouring your hair. This is because once a client has experienced a reaction to hair colour dye, the immune system 'remembers' the chemical and will launch a defense reaction the next time you are exposed to it.

CASE STUDY SIX

Anonymous

The way it was back then....

A new client came in for a colouring service. This was in 2008, and we were not skin testing clients. I do not know of any salons that were at that time. We asked the client some questions about her hair and her answers gave us no contra-indications or reasons to believe that we should not proceed with a service. We did not document the consultation.

All is not as appears

As we proceeded with the service it was becoming apparent that something was not right. The colour we had applied was OK on the roots but was not processing as it should on the mid lengths and ends. We decided to apply a mild bleach solution to the mid lengths and ends to move the level a couple of shades so that we could reapply the target formula. When we applied the bleach solution the hair became very hot, we immediately rinsed it off. The end result was that the roots were lighter than the mid lengths and ends and the hair was dry (not breaking) where we had applied the bleach.

What did we do wrong?

We did not charge the client, she made it clear she did not get what she wanted and so was not prepared to pay. We offered for her to come in the next week so that we could put a treatment on and seek some advice from our colour house on how to proceed further. She made an appointment but did not show. A

couple of weeks later we got a letter from a no-win no-fee and we passed it to our insurers.

Breach of terms

They sent a loss adjuster to interview us about what happened. A couple of weeks after this we received a letter from the insurance company to say that we were in breach of our policy because we did not follow manufacturers instructions, namely skin testing and strand testing, and consequently they would not be covering the claim. We spoke on the telephone with the insurance company and took some legal advice and discovered that the insurance company could do this. Furthermore the insurance company made clear to us that unless we followed manufacturers instructions we would not be covered on future services. This meant that we had to skin test every client, every service. I cannot put into words how we felt at that time. We were like rabbits in headlights in the salon – our regular clients could not understand why we had to suddenly start skin testing them. We lost some clients over it. New clients would often go to another salon, as it was more convenient for them. We felt singled out.

Settlement

Meanwhile the no-win no-fee wrote to us with the details of the claim and advised us to appoint a solicitor. The worry was unbelievable. The NHF legal line was brilliant. They advised us that we should settle the claim; we did not have a leg to stand on in court. We could deal directly with the no-win no-fee, and that maybe they would accept a settlement if we dealt with it quickly. Whilst it was not what we wanted to hear at least we knew what we had to do. The claim was for £12000, we went to the offices of the no-win no-fee for a meeting. All I want to say about it is they agreed to £10000 if we paid within two months. They said we could make a proposal to pay in installments but that would have to be for the full amount. We just wanted to move on so we went to the bank for a loan and we solved it that way. We believe the client got £2000 of the £10000.

How things have changed

It was an expensive and painful lesson but for us every cloud does have a silver lining. We carry out services in full compliance of the manufacturers instructions. We have taken advice from Debbie and document everything. We skin test every client every service. Today we have clients come to us because they heard how vigilant and thorough we are. We offer a free strand testing service for clients. It helps us manage clients' expectations, plan service times and quote accurate prices. We have learned a lot from strand testing, not least of all how often clients are not able to give us accurate information about the history of their hair. We recently had a stylist leave after only a few months with us because she felt our policies and systems were 'too much'. What a shame she did not want to rise to our standard.

Debbie's comments

Experience is a ruthless teacher

This is a valuable lesson for us all to learn from. A £10000 lesson in their case, and that does not take into consideration the worry and angst

suffered. I have seen the trichologist report for this case and it catalogues a series of assumptions of things that did not happen, but unfortunately in the event there was little documentation it is difficult to defend the case. What's more, defending a case without insurance can be an expensive experience. The case study in Chapter 13 is compelling reading regarding fighting without insurance cover. In the trichologist report there were numerous assumptions and accusations that were not correct. I reiterate the only way to counter these assumptions and accusations is with documented evidence.

What is your policy for skin testing?

'A new client came in for a colouring service. This was in 2008, and we were not skin testing clients. I do not know of any salons that were at that time.'

I recently did a little research by calling 7 salons in a town presenting myself as a prospective client new to the area. I asked about their policy on skin testing. I had 7 different answers ranging from the salon that stated 'we require a test 48 hours before every service, you will need to come to the salon' to 'do you colour your hair regularly?' 'Yes every six weeks' I replied, 'always in a salon?' they asked, 'yes' I replied. 'You will be fine' they said. 'So I do not require a test?' I asked 'no you will be fine' the reply.

And one salon who simply replied, 'we don't do skin testing'. Thank goodness for our industry that it was I researching in this instance and not the TV production crew from BBC program X-Ray (South Wales). They sent a 12 year old undercover to see how salon's would react to her request to colour her hair for Episode 5, Series 7. Just one salon acted correctly on guidance in manufacturers instructions regarding young people under 16.

Strand testing

'As we proceeded with the service it was becoming apparent that something was not right.'

We have all been there, you have planned a service and something is interfering with your plan. What's more, you have no idea what is happening because you do not know the hair history. Whenever you have a complex colour service or a new client complete a skin test, documented consultation, strand test and technical method of work. This allows you to plan more accurately the service time on the day, the cost, and the products needed. There may still be problems during the service because you have only strand tested a sample, but you have done all you can to deliver the service in a professional way.

Void insurance

'They sent a loss adjuster to interview us about what happened. A couple of weeks after this we received a letter from the insurance company to say that we were in breach of our policy'

A loss adjuster's job is to ascertain who is at fault and therefor who is liable. If an insurance company can reject a claim they will. It is as simple as that. Chapter 1 – Hair Industry Regulation? We have it............. And here it is, if a hairdresser does not follow manufacturers guidelines, the standards set, (I would advise following NVQ 2 and 3 guidelines) and take appropriate care when undertaking services they will be at fault should something go wrong. If a stylist is employed the responsibility is the salon owners to hold liability insurance and to uphold professional standards in the salon.

Deal with claims quickly

'The NHF legal line was brilliant. They advised us that we should settle the claim; we did not have a leg to stand on in court. We could deal directly with the no-win no-fee, and that maybe they would accept a settlement if we dealt with it quickly.'

I am a huge fan of the NHF, the legal advice I have had from them over the years has been invaluable. I am aware that some salon owners can get frustrated because they feel the NHF legal helpline advice can lean towards the employees favour in employment legal issues. It is important to understand that you own your business and you make your decisions. On employment issues I tend to take advice from NHF, ACAS, sometimes an independent HR solicitor and then I make my own decision. There are other options; you may choose to use a HR company who supports you from contract to court on employment issues. All are good, most important is that you have support in this area.

Justice?

'We believe the client got £2000 of the £10000.'

This is most typical from the cases I have seen. Compare this case study to the one in Chapter 13 and you can understand why the insurance companies pay out on claims. However please remember that insurance companies are

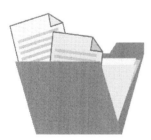 keen to make a stand against spurious claims where they have the ability to do so. If you have documentation, photos, witnesses and a passion to fight you have half a chance of pushing the insurance company to fight the case to court. Our industry needs this to happen to take the focus away from us. You may be aware that over the last few years the claims industry has had an aggressive focus on PPI claims. You may also be aware, probably from radio, TV and media advertising that the

deadline for PPI claims is 29th August 2019. Here is an interesting question to ponder – who/what will the claims industry focus on after that date?

Commercial decisions

'Today we have clients come to us because they heard how vigilant and thorough we are.'

I understand that the policies, procedures, documentation, standards and training can seem daunting and a pain in the neck. It takes time, discipline and money. But on the flip side, I know a salon can enjoy many benefits beyond protection from insurance claims. Do you want your salon to stand out from the crowd? Do you want to attract clients who really care about their hair and are prepared to pay for professional services? I believe the biggest problem we have in dealing with the challenges presented is the pressure on prices and the competition we are up against because the client has a lot of choice when it comes to choosing how and where to get their hair done. Rise to the challenge and reap the benefits.

Case Study Seven

Anonymous

A normal day

A client had been coming to the salon for 3 years having a colour service every 8 weeks. We performed the colour service as we normally would using exactly the same colours. 10 days after the service the client went to the Dr as she had experienced some itching and swelling on her face. Her Dr asked her some questions and made the assumption that her irritation could be from colouring her hair. He informed her she had an allergic reaction to the colour and he/she should get in touch with the hairdresser. The client made contact with us and we informed her that is it not usual to suffer from an allergic reaction 10 days after a colour application, but as a colour responsible salon we would do our very best to help her discover what was the cause. We offered her dermatologist assessment - all costs covered by us. The client had the dermatologist assessment and we were informed that the results are confidential and cannot be shared with us. A few weeks later we received a letter from a no-win no-fee solicitor to tell us they were representing our client and been instructed to seek a claim against us. This claim is still be dealt with by our insurers.

Debbie's comments

Hair colour reactions typically occur between 6 - 48 hours after exposure to colour. There is a difference between reaction, irritation and sensitivity. Drs make notes on their patients record and these comments become, for a Judge, compelling evidence. It would be interesting to see the dermatologists report, and if the client relies on it in court the salon will get to see it. But I suspect if it is not conclusive in supporting the client's claim it may never see the light of day. I suspect the solicitors will rely on a trichologist report that will once again accuse the hairdressers of poor application, leaving the color on too long, not being properly trained/qualified, not properly supervised etc. etc. The insurance company will have to make a decision on how far to push the claim. How much to invest in it, time of the insurance company, solicitors time, court costs, barristers fees and so on. Unless the salon owner is really motivated to see it go to court it will likely be settled. The client will get a bit and the no-win no-fee will get more. The salon owners insurance will go up. All our insurance will go up. And the claims industry goes fishing for the next claim, advertising in magazines, on the internet, social media and radio. I apologise if I make it sound depressing, but I do so for a reason. The insurance company will cover this claim; the salon owner and the team have done nothing wrong. There is a business to run, clients to serve, hair to style, lives to live. This claim is what we pay insurance for and whilst it may not sit right from a justice point of view – sometimes you just have to let go and move on. Sometimes you just have to trust the Universe.

Case Study Eight

Marguerite Marshall

Looking for services on the cheap

On the afternoon of 25th October 2011 a lady we will call WD came into our salon to enquire about the price of Hi-Lights and a cut and blow dry with a mid priced stylist. She spoke to our assistant manager Carole and said she could not afford the cost, but was desperate to have her hair done. WD then went on to ask if we did any training sessions at a reduced cost? She carried on chatting to Carole for quite some time about different things, thus making Carole think she was a very polite and nice person who Carole kind of felt sorry for. The following morning Carole explained to me about WD, she asked if we could accommodate WD and explained how she just wanted a scattering of foils, to break up her regrowth of around 5 months. So we decided to let Emma our almost qualified level 3 stylist do it for her, as the salon was quiet.

Follow your instinct

WD arrived a couple of hours later - I was busy with clients. Call it intuition but I straightaway had a feeling about WD, 30 years in the industry...... you just know! I asked Carole and Emma to both give her individual consultations, as I would also, so we all knew what WD's expectations were for the colour service. During a consultation WD was asked if she had any previous skin irritations to colour or if she ever had a henna tattoo. She answered NO. Emma was a Level 3 student at Loughborough College and they did not require a patch test for any type of colour service at that time. Emma, Carole and myself all agreed that a scattering T Section of Hi-Lights using tint in colour wraps was to be used and Carole would pass up to Emma through the whole process.

As they started the service, WD asked to be sat near the door as she said she didn't like the usual salon smells and the colour odour. Our salon is large and airy - alarm bells were ringing in my head!!!

So far so good

All through the development time Emma and Carole sat chatting to WD, she was never left alone. Once the colour process time was up Emma took the colour wraps off (no bleeding and a perfect colour was achieved). Emma went on to cut and dry WD's Hair.

Once she was finished I asked if she was pleased with the service and result, she was so pleased she gave Emma a £5 tip as a thank you on top of the nominal fee of £30.

Here comes trouble

A couple of hours later WD called and spoke with Carole and asked for more HI-Lights, she asked to come in that afternoon (the same day). We were busy by then and agreed to book in the following week. I told Carole there would be a charge of £10 for the extra work as when she left she was fully pleased with the result. She seemed miffed by this and I was miffed at her wasting our time, she agreed and the appointment was made. About an hour later she called again and asked if Carole could do it TODAY, as she wanted it done TODAY. Carole explained we were all busy with clients, she then said she wanted her money refunded so she could go elsewhere. I refused.

Reaction

An hour later she walked into the salon and told Carole she had applied hydrocortisone cream on her face and neck, as she was experiencing

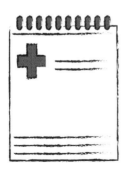

burning. Carole was also an advanced trained beauty therapist and explained to WD that hydrocortisone cream is a steroid cream and should only be applied after a Drs recommendation for use on the face. She showed Carole her neck and face and there was NO SIGN of any irritation. She then stormed out of the salon. Within an hour WD returned, waving a prescription around and shouting 'I've had an allergic reaction.' I then excused myself from my client to deal with WD. I asked her to calm down, stop shouting and to tell me what she wanted. She said 'I WANT MY MONEY BACK.' I refused because her hair was exactly as she had requested and was absolutely beautiful, a complete makeover of the mess she walked in with. She carried on shouting and I told her to leave and opened the door, she walked out and shouted "I'll see you in court".

No-win no-fee

A few weeks later a letter arrived form a no-win no-fee solicitor stating that they were acting for WD. They were suing us due to the fact that a trainee who was not properly supervised throughout the procedure undertook the service. WD said she had sustained burns to her face and neck and the colour was inadequate! I was shocked but I guess I expected a come back from WD. I admit I did not take this seriously and left it in the hands of my partner to deal with. We were at that time going through a messy break up, I was fighting him through solicitors after a 23 year relationship. We were not on good speaking terms. This was a huge mistake. He eventually spoke to the NHF legal team and didn't tell me so I was unaware of the conversation. Our insurers refused to take up the claim because we had not followed manufacturers instructions (not patch tested). NHF would have helped us after our Insurers refused, but by the time I took up the case I was out of the timescale set by NHF due to being unaware of the previous conversations with my partner.

The situation escalates

In 2015 I received a court placement hearing, which was the first I'd heard for some time about the case. I attended and was told by the Judge that because her no-win no-fee solicitor had upped the claim only 2 days prior to the hearing, he had no choice but to place the case in Fast Track - her

solicitors were playing the system. The Judge asked the no-win no-fee to disclose evidence in the form of photographic and medical records 3 months before and 3 months after the alleged incident. NONE OF THIS EVIDENCE WAS EVER DISCLOSED! We chased and chased through my solicitor, I believe the no-win no-fee played the game and I was just not wise to any of this. This was costing me financially everything I had.

Was my gut feeling right?

I decided to do a bit of research on WD myself. I followed my gut feeling and I called and asked local salons if they had any history with her. I found 3 salons that knew her and she had been banned from them all for nuisance complaining until she got a refund! They all gave me a statement. With my new evidence how could this fraud, which is what it was, not be thrown out of court? I decided to call one more salon...... She was still having her hair coloured in the next village! They used the exact same colour brand on her; they told me she had a recent patch test and NEVER HAD A REACTION! I had a new urge to whip this woman's ass. How could she not react to a patch test or a colour service if she was allergic to colour?

The case continues

We were still pressing for the evidence the Judge requested. Finally medical records came to light, BUT the months before and after the incident were not available due to a corrupt file???? The only relevant bit disclosed was the Drs notes on the day she was in the salon! WD had a rash that could have been caused by a hair colourant. This note was the bullet my barrister delivered in his report that he did about a week before the court date. He stated the Judge would rely on the fact no patch test was done and the Drs note. Even though NO PHOTOGRAPHIC EVIDENCE HAD BEEN submitted despite the Judges' request. I'd fought for the past year for nothing. This whole horrible experience had to come to an end, and I was near to broke and completely deflated.

UNBELIEVABLE BUT TRUE

At this point I had a coffee with Debbie Digby, how I wished I'd contacted her before. I was not experienced in any of this and believed telling the truth would shine through and WD's LIES would be revealed. I had a long hard think - I couldn't afford to lose. I'd just beat my Ex in court and got the business to myself. I couldn't risk losing. I had nothing else other than my business of 12 years. So I agreed to settle. WD was

paid £1000.00 and I waited for the no-win no-fee solicitor's bill to be delivered. Their bill came to an eye watering £28000.00, which included their 100% success fee. If this story is not a reason to protect yourself and your business of the fraudulent claims in our industry I don't know what is. A patch test takes seconds and costs pennies. WD cost me near £50000.00 including my own costs........ A HORROR STORY, very real and more common than you may think.

Debbie's comments

I have no doubt you join me in my sadness that Mags experienced this. It makes you wonder if there is any justice in the World. I am so grateful to Mags for agreeing to share her story for the benefit of all who read this book. I do not feel the desire to comment further on Mags case which was exasperated further by her personal circumstance. The book documents enough information for salons to implement in order to prevent and defend claims. I think her story is compelling enough. Suffice to say - today her salon is still providing fabulous services to the clients, she is happy in her new marriage to a wonderfully supportive man and her daughter has been emotionally moved to train as a barrister so she may positively influence the legal process.

Social Media

The internet is a giant conversation everyone and anyone can join. Depending on what someone has to say about you or your business determines whether that is a good or bad thing. Love it or hate it, it is imperative a business is interacting on social media in some way. A salon owner recently told me he was not on social media, I showed him that whilst he personally was not logging on and engaging, there are indeed  references to his business and pictures of him. He signed up to at least monitor if nothing else. Before social media, negative experiences would stay within a circle of friends. Now stories of poor customer service or disappointing experiences can spread quickly online. Likewise a good campaign can reach a targeted audience fast and with little or no budget. So we are to understand and accept that there are two sides to social media, and it is important we are in control of what impacts us and our business. This chapter is not about the marketing opportunities, rather the legal aspects we may face.

A refund - or else?

Respond to client complaints quickly and impartially. Apologise for any inconvenience – 'Thank you for letting me know you are not happy, I am sorry you feel this way' – there is no admittance of any wrongdoing in this sentence, but it demonstrates to the client that you are not defensive. Find out what the client wants and why she thinks this is reasonable. 'We take complaints like this seriously and I want to change your experience and meet the expectations you feel we have failed to reach. Please explain to me what you asked for and how we have not met your request'. Once we get into a dialogue with the client we can find out all the facts. Has she got pictures and what do they look like? Has she suffered an injury? Is the finished look not up to standard? I have seen complaints published on social media that have been shared thousands of times to the detriment of a business (and a stylists pride and confidence). On the other hand I have seen complaints published that have attracted little attention. If you find yourself the victim of a social media post or poor review your response (or lack of it) can make all the difference to the way the information is received by the audience. I recently had a client demand a refund and state if she did not get it by 5pm she would be left with no alternative than to take action. We gathered information from her, her records, the stylist and the manager. It seemed by her own admission that there was nothing wrong with the colour or the service, but she was not happy with the cut. We ascertained that she had some pictures, and we asked her to send them to us. I could see that whilst she was not happy with the cut, it was her preference rather that a technically poor haircut. We weighed up the risk, we offered her, by email two appointments with a top stylist as a gesture of goodwill to give us the chance to change her experience but refused her request to a refund. We had a plan should she publish the photos on social media they were not that bad and we would publish the response to demonstrate our reasonableness in

dealing with her dissatisfaction. On this occasion we managed the situation well.

Shout about your great work

There is no doubt a lot of beautiful hair coming out of your salon, tell the World about it. Make it professional though. Use a backdrop, good lighting, have the team learn how to take the best pictures to show of their work in the best way. Build a presence. Should you be unfortunate to have something nasty posted, your previous history helps to demonstrate it is not the normal standard for your salon and is a one off. You can then respond with empathy and a genuine concern for the clients dissatisfaction and rectify the situation or at least diffuse it.

Protect your business

Pictures taken in the salon by employees are the property of the business. The employee is being paid to carry out work on behalf of the salon. If you have pictures taken with a backdrop it makes it easy to restrict the use of those pictures should an employee leave your business and try to use the salons work to promote themselves in another setting. Be specific about what employees can and cannot post on social media regarding work activities, and also give advice about what they post out of work. It is important for all to understand our digital footprint. Once we have put something to social media it is a footprint that cannot be erased. It is there forever retrievable in varying degrees. I have seen salons and stylists post on Facebook 'cancellation for a colour this afternoon - grab it while you can'. This could potentially cause a problem if you have to prove that you follow skin testing directives. I have no doubt all salon owners know the power of social media in monitoring employees social activities and in both chapter 7 and Feathers Colchester court case we can appreciate the power it yields.

Manufacturers Instructions and Standard Procedures

Claims industry

You may be aware that over the last few years the claims industry has had an aggressive focus on PPI claims. You may also be aware, probably from radio, TV and media advertising that the deadline for PPI claims is 29th August 2019. Here is an interesting question to ponder – who/what will the claims industry focus on after that date? Thomas Cook has recently addressed the problem of gastric illness claims by tightening up their compensation procedures and taking legal action against  fraudsters. I understand part of the change they have made is investigating and dealing with claims in house rather than just passing claims over to their insurance company. Maybe the rising cost of their insurance has influenced this decision? Or maybe complying with stricter terms and conditions from the insurance companies has brought about change? Whatever the reasons the comparisons to our industry are clear – the difference is that we are an industry of over 35000 independently owned salons with approx. 94000 self employed, an industry largely fragmented, dealing with these issues unregulated and independently.

Manufacturers instructions

As a young hairdresser I don't think I pulled the instructions out of the box. Funny little leaflets with tiny letters printed on super thin paper like pages of a Bible. About as interesting as nothing! I admit that my first interest was once I was working as brand manager for a large colour manufacturer. I came to appreciate the importance of the instructions as a tool to protect the manufacturer and distributor. Then I realised the importance of the instructions for the hairdresser and have been teaching and preaching to hairstylists about policies, protocols and procedures since then.

Skin/patch testing

It is a great frustration that we cannot have a standard skin test that every colour manufacturer, distributor, hairdresser and colour consumer can use. It would be so much easier wouldn't it? And consistent? Suffice to say – read the manufacturers instructions, consult the companies educators and representatives, ask your insurance company, read industry approved text books and websites. Please do not just follow what others do, or take advice from social media. Record your skin tests and have clients sign to say they have had a skin test. It is hard to believe that people would lie, but they do.

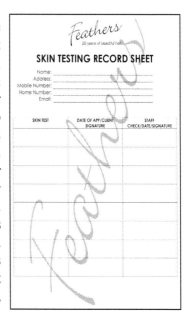

Strand testing

My advice on strand testing is that if you are doing a routine service with a regular client it is not necessary. If you have a complex service, a new service for a regular client or a new client - strand test. You can strand test on or off the head depending on what you are testing. If it is off the head you should cut samples of hair from inconspicuous places, preferably in a couple of different parts of the head to test if the hair is different at the sides from the back. If you are seeing the client for a skin test you can take strands days ahead of time. Some strand tests only take a short amount of time – maybe a couple of hours. Some strand testing is taking place during a service. This is to monitor the service and should not be confused with the ability to pre plan a service with a degree of accuracy.

Incompatibility test

Take a small piece of hair and put it into a solution as directed in the manufacturers instructions for the product you are going to use. You are checking that there is no adverse reaction to the hair. This could be seen by the hair or lotion heating up, changing an unexpected colour or bubbling.

Porosity test

Porosity is a measure of the compactness of the cuticle layers of the hair. When the cuticle is raised water passes easily in and out of the hair shaft. The result is that the hair feels dry and rough and looks frizzy. When the cuticle scales are tightly closed – for example in white hair – the hair becomes resistant. To test for porosity take one strand of hair that is clean with no added products and put into a clear container of room temperature water. If the hair floats it has low porosity, if it settles midway it is normal and if it sinks it has high porosity.

Elasticity/Stretch/Pull test

Take approximately 10 clean wet hairs between your index finger and your thumb on both hands, one inch apart. Now pull the hair and observe the stretch. It should easily stretch one third (to an inch and a third) and immediately return to its former one-inch. If it is difficult to stretch and appears to be 'stiff' it needs moisture for flexibility. If it stretches more than one third and appears 'baggy' when it returns it needs protein for strength.

Under 16 year olds

Since November 2011 the EU Commission has recommended that all oxidative and non-oxidative coloration products carry new guidelines that state, "This product is not intended for use on persons under the age of 16." This is to protect children from allergic reactions. What I think is a real shame about this directive is 16 year olds will continue to colour their hair and their first experience will be at home. They will turn to salons when it goes wrong – and if they are under age a salon will not be able to help with a colour correction.

Previous reactions

Once someone has had a reaction to hair colour they should not colour their hair again. Not in foils, not off the scalp, not at all. If you read carefully the manufacturers instructions you are cautioned – do not use this product if you have ever experienced any reaction after colouring your hair. This is because once a client has experienced a reaction to hair colour dye, the immune system 'remembers' the chemical and will launch a defense reaction the next time you are exposed to it.

The above is by no means an exhaustive list – but it is intended to give an indication of some procedures that may be followed.

Finally

This book is for information purposes only and does not constitute legal advice. It is recommended that specific professional advice be sought before acting on any of the information given.

Printed in Great Britain
by Amazon